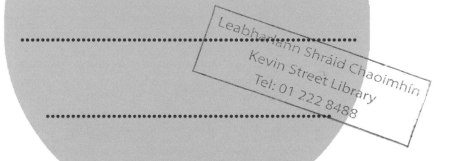

This Orchard book belongs to

....

....

ORCHARD BOOKS
338 Euston Road, London NW1 3BH
Orchard Books Australia
Level 17/207 Kent Street, Sydney, NSW 2000

First published in 2011 by Orchard Books
First published in paperback in 2012

ISBN 978 1 40831 197 4

Text and illustrations © Alison Murray 2011

A CIP catalogue record for this book is
available from the British Library.

10 9 8 7 6 5 4 3 2 1

Printed in China

Orchard Books is a division of
Hachette Children's Books,
an Hachette UK company.

www.hachette.co.uk

ONE TWO

That's My Shoe!

Alison Murray

ORCHARD

One . . .

2

Two

That's my shoe!

3

Three . . .

Four

Out the door!

5

XXXXX

Five . . .

6

Six

Doggie tricks!

Seven . . .

7

8

Eight

Through the gate!

Nine . . .

Ten

10

Shooo!

Friends again!

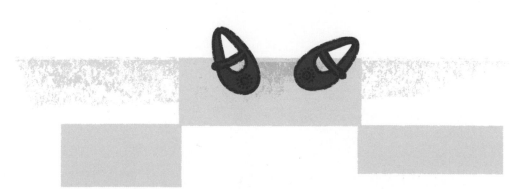